TALES FROM THE SADDLE

Compiled by

ALVIN STARDUST

Stanley Paul
London Melbourne Sydney Auckland Johannesberg

Stanley Paul & Co. Ltd

An imprint of the Hutchinson Publishing Group

17–21 Conway Street, London W1P 6JD

Hutchinson Publishing Group (Australia) Pty Ltd
PO Box 496, 16–22 Church Street, Hawthorne, Melbourne,
Victoria 3122

Hutchinson Group (NZ) Ltd
32–34 View Road, PO Box 40-086, Glenfield, Auckland 10

Hutchinson Group (SA) Pty Ltd
PO Box 337, Bergvlei 2012, South Africa

First published 1984
© Alvin Stardust 1984

Set in Plantin by BookEns, Saffron Walden, Essex

Printed and bound in Great Britain by Anchor Brendon Ltd,
Tiptree, Essex

ISBN 0 09 155190 0

Contents

Foreword

There is a great mixture of stories in Tales from the Saddle. Some painful, some imaginative, some sad and some highly entertaining and I am most grateful to Alvin Stardust for the effort that was no doubt involved in gathering these stories together. I did not think it was worth my contributing because most of these sort of occasions that have happened to me have already been recorded for posterity, even if the script is often imaginary. There is one incident that sticks in my mind which was not witnessed by anybody and could be entitled "complacency can damage your health".

In the summer holidays, I would always go out in the evening to bring the ponies in from the field. I would put their head-collars on and ride bareback and lead the others, no problem. This particular evening I was only bringing in two. I'd done my usual of bicycling down to the stables, left the bicycle leaning against the wall beside the door, collected the headcollars and walked up to the field, caught the two animals and jumped on my old pony and led the other one. All went as normal till I reached the stables. There, for reasons which only horses know, the one that I was leading decided to shy at my bicycle and stopped dead, my old pony kept going and walked through the door into his box and turned round to have his head collar taken off to be greeted by the sight of his erstwhile rider sitting on the cobblestones outside the door due to an equally inexplicable reaction which had persuaded me to let go of the wrong bit of string, so that I was pulled unerringly straight off my pony's backside and landed unceremoniously on my own backside still attached to the animal who had started this unnecessary chain of events by either his failing eyesight, or perhaps a sudden loss of memory as to the shape of a bicycle. I looked round to see if this

7

"incident" had been witnessed, was heartily relieved to find that it had not as there was no-one about and then I continued as if nothing had happened. Somehow, it was the splendid isolation of the incident, the incredulous expression on my pony's face and no doubt the cobblestones, that made such an impression on me.

Perhaps if any readers feel they have an equine related story they have an urge to tell, they might send them to the Save the Children Fund and we could produce a second edition of Tales from the Saddle.

In this country we enjoy horses for the pleasure they give in many different ways. In some parts of the world the horse is still a vital part of society, where there is no clean water, sanitation, insufficient food and probably no medical care. In donating the proceeds of this original book to the Save the Children Fund, the fund will be able to continue to give some of the world's neediest children some of those things we take so much for granted.

Anne.

Her Royal Highness
The Princess Anne
Mrs Mark Phillips, GCVO
President The Save the Children Fund

Norman Thelwell

Artist and wit

When I was in India, I was staying at a place called Naini Tal in the hills. It was an extinct volcano, with a lake down the middle, and the only flat road was round the lake. The rest of the houses and buildings in the town were up on the cliff faces. They used to hire out horses down by the lake and, since I was staying heaven knows how far up the mountain, I hired a horse.

We trotted happily enough round the lake until we got to where I had to go up the slope. I thought, 'These horses are very wise,' since this one seemed about to give up. So I sort of 'heeled' it into a gallop, and when it hit the slope it went absolutely crazy, careering up this sheer face at a maniacal rate. It was a kind of hairpin road, round terrible corners, and I was totally unable to control the horse. When we arrived at the small hotel where we were staying (I was in the army at the time), a group of my mates were standing on the hotel balcony and saw me coming. I don't know whether you've ever read the poem 'John Gilpin', but it was like that. They saw us coming hell for leather and were cheering like mad. I couldn't stop the horse so it went way on past the hotel and continued until we were right up on the crest. I was terrified, only just holding on.

From the top you could see the foothills of the Himalayas, and terrible drops on either side. My mount stopped when it got there. Thank God. Otherwise we'd have gone down into the jungle on the other side. I turned its nose back again, and we started down, but then we did the same thing again. We went sailing past the hotel until finally I stopped the creature down by the lake. An Indian came along who owned the horses and took the thing off me, and I finally went up on Shanks's pony. What did amuse me was that when I got back to the hotel (of course I took a hell of a lot of bantering from the boys, who were falling about laughing), I felt very uncomfortable, and found that my underpants had been ripped completely in two, so there was half down each leg.

Cyril Smith

Prominent Parliamentary figure

I've been fond of horses all my life, though riding has never been a hobby of mine! I remember many many years ago, deciding to take a ride in a landau in Killarney Ireland. I mounted the step, got seated and the dear old horse said, 'Neigh, neigh', which I took to mean 'Nay, Nay!'!

Jimmy Savile

BR. PR

Horses and I are strangers, but pit ponies and I are the best of friends, since I drove one for nearly three years. It was during the time I worked at Waterloo Colliery in Leeds and my pony and I shared many hours of darkness and quite back-breaking work as the coal was 'hand got' as we called it in those pre-mechanical days.

To get to the coal face, me and my nag had to walk some three miles, part of which was down a deep drift with a gradient of one in four. Coming back, the drift reared up like the north face of Everest and it was a joy for me to hang on to the pony's tackle and get pulled up the steep slope. My animal had different ideas and, even though it was very friendly most of the time and quite prepared to eat all my sandwiches, would sod off at a great rate of knots at the bottom of the drift in the hope that it would outrun me before I could catch hold of its tow chain.

Over three years, the score was about square and on the days that the pony won, it would wait for me at the top and snort all over me with a 'that's fixed you today' attitude.

Don't tell me that our four-legged friends do not have a sense of humour, as his was evil.

Suggs
Madness

When I was little and in short trousers I remember having a go on a horse one day after I'd been all morning collecting conkers. So my pockets were crammed full of them when I set off on this horse. I thought it would be best if I didn't act scared but showed who was in charge, so I did. However, so did the horse – and he won. After dragging me along a pebbledashed wall and out into the fields, he stopped dead at a hedge and dumped me over the top. Of course, it had been raining hard for days and I went head first into about six inches of mud. The skin had been ripped off my leg, my clothes were torn to shreds by the thorns in the hedge and I was knocked almost unconscious. When the onlookers found me and I came to, the first thing I said was, 'Where are me conkers?'

Linda McCartney
Wings

Wings were touring America for the first time. We rented a house in Dallas and rehearsed in Fort Worth. I'd decided I wanted more than anything an Appaloosa. Appaloosas are the original American Indian pony. There was a Walt Disney film about them recently. I asked the promoter of the tour, 'Do you know of any Appaloosas? I want the Indian type though. They usually cross them with thoroughbred Quarter horses for the colour. But they don't have the temperament – you know, that Indian frame of mind.'

So they showed me all these fancy horses. No way. They weren't what I was talking about.

We used to drive from Dallas to Fort Worth, and one day I saw this Appaloosa exactly the way I dreamed it. He was in a field like a paddock, with a palomino. We drove the route every day, but I didn't see him the next. Paul was driving, there was just the two of us, and the following day he was there again. I thought, 'That's it.' He was pure black with a white blanket over his bottom end and big black spots. So we pulled off the freeway and we finally found this little farmhouse that said 'Lucky Spot Appaloosas'.

I didn't want a gelding, or a stallion. I only really wanted a mare. I told the old farmhand about the one I'd just seen and he said, 'I've put him away.' I'd just missed him. But he took us to see this little stallion. The farmer didn't want to sell him as his kids loved the horse. So I said I understood and we were happy to have seen him. Anyway, to cut a long story short, they had the other horses and very kindly sold him to us. Afterwards we became very friendly with the family and the kids come to the concerts. But the horse was wonderful. A lovely, lovely temperament, so beautiful, and I realized my dream: he lives with us now in England.

Paul McCartney
Wings

Well, there was a time when they were trying to find a horse for me, and not knowing anything about horses, I tried anything that came along. And this huge Black Beauty type of thoroughbred stallion was put before me. So I thought, 'Well, they must know,' and I took it out on to Farnham Common where the horsy people were. And the bloody horse ran away with me. I was pulling on its mouth shouting, 'Stop, stop!' Course, it wasn't stopping, it was just picking up speed. Going terrifically across the Common. The only thing I could work out was that there was wasteland ahead that looked like being a thirty-mile gallop if he kept going straight. So I saw this bush in the middle of the Common and I just headed directly for the bush. We ran right into it. It stopped him, eventually. That was pretty frightening, but I advise anyone in a similar predicament to just run straight into the middle of the nearest bush.

I've gradually learned a little more about horses now and I find that some kind of friendship with the animal is a big help, even if it's only brushing him before you go out. That way the horse knows that you're not out to kill it. Before this discovery I always just used to jump on, ride like Harvey Smith for half an hour and jump off again. Linda is very interested in Appaloosas, and the fella she bought is a stallion, so we have been trying to see if we can breed Appaloosas with a couple of others we've got. The first baby we ever had was a lovely foal, but you couldn't have said she was an Appaloosa because she didn't really have a spot on her. Still, that was OK, we thought. You can't do anything about that. The second foal we had by the stallion got our hopes up again. Pitch black! Not a mark on him. They were both lovely horses, but again we felt like sending them back to ask for a rebate. 'Where are the spots?' Linda was philosophical. She said, 'Well, you can't guarantee it.'

By the time we had the third foal we were half expecting to walk down there and see a chestnut mare or something. We looked in the morning he was born, and there lying in all the hay was this beautiful little colt, with a blanket of spots, absolutely typical Appaloosa markings. Third time lucky.

So we called him 'Blanket'.

Harvey Smith
Show jumper extraordinaire

I was in a jump-off with a fella one day. He was so bloody slow, a snail could beat 'im. And I go round on a good 'oss and I fly. Then all of a sudden 'e goos in on 'is bloody snail, and 'alfway round, clock stopped. Anyway, 'e keeps gooin' and finishes 'is round, and they give 'is time out faster than mine. So I shot up t'judges' box. I said, 'Bloody 'ell, how the 'ell did you manage to get a time like that?' I said, 'That bloody thing couldn't win a donkey derby let alone a good 'un of 'is class.'

Any road, the fella told me 'ow 'e'd judged it. You know, when clock stopped. 'E leant back over, got 'is watch out of 'is pocket, and then 'e clicked it on and then 'e clicked it off when the 'oss went through t'finish. Then 'e added the two lots together and that was 'is total time. But 'e 'adn't allowed for about fifteen seconds in t'middle while 'e were leanin' over. And I said, 'Well if you judge it like that, that's bloody fiddling.' So then 'e went on about stewards, one thing and another, what 'e wasn't gooin' to do to me. I said, 'Well, what should I do in a case like this? Should I withdraw?' He said, 'No, but your bloody father should have done thirty years since.'

Robert Powell

Thespian

It was about 1971, and I'd never been on a horse before in my life, though I'd been on a donkey when I was a kid. Well, I was asked to play Shelley in a thing for 'Omnibus' about the life of the poet, which involved going around Italy on location for eight weeks. One of the locations was on a lido in Venice, and I looked at the script and it said, 'Byron and Shelley on horseback on the sands,' so I said to the director, 'You know I don't really ride.' 'Oh it's nothing complicated,' he said. 'I wouldn't worry about it if I were you.' I persisted, 'You know, I haven't actually ever been on a horse.' 'No, no, no, it'll be fine; we'll get you a docile animal, something calm, and you won't have to do anything at all.' So I said, 'OK, fine.'

On the day, we arrive there and this enormous black stallion is led up, and a small dumpy mare, so I assumed that the dumpy mare was my horse. I was given the black stallion. I said, 'What's it called?' 'Papa Satan.' I said, 'What does that mean?' 'Devil's tongue.' 'Oh, that's nice.' I told them no, I couldn't do it, and the director said, 'All right, just get on it and let's take it from there.' So I get on the horse and of course what directors in general must realize but this one didn't, is that actors are mimicks, and although I'd never been on a horse, I'd watched enough John Wayne films to know how to sit on one, with my knees in, my heels down, and my back straight. And they all exclaimed, 'Oh, you can ride!' The horse is at this point standing still. I said, 'No! But I know how to look as if I can.' They told me fine, all we want to do is this one shot of you, trotting or galloping past the camera into the sea, and I said, 'Pardon!' So they turned to the interpreter and asked, 'Does this horse like water?' 'Oh, he like-a-de-water,' was the immediate response. So I put in, 'Are you sure he likes the water?' 'He like-a-de-water, every morning he like-a-de-water.'

So these two horses are put up at the back of this beach. The

17

camera is set up, action is called, we charge down the sand. I have absolutely no control now at all, and we are heading straight into the sea. Byron's horse gallops straight in, with great glee; my horse actually turns at right angles at the edge and I don't, and I come off backwards and skid down the beach on my arse facing camera into the water and then grind to a halt with my head whipping back, clunk. So on film is this figure skidding across the sand into the sea on his backside shouting 'F........!' Somewhere in the BBC archives that still exists. Sound and Vision.

Ringo Starr
Singer and actor

Every time I get on a horse, it seems to want to take me away somewhere. Not long ago I bought myself a horse and I've called her Dolly Parton. 'Cos she's got a lovely smile.

Frank Hardy
All-Australian story-telling champion

A few years ago, in Australia, there was a boom in pub cricket. The drinkers at one hotel in a suburb or town would challenge the drinkers at another hotel to a friendly game. The publicans would supply two or three eighteen-gallon kegs of beer and a good time would be had by all.

Of course, the quality of the cricket would decline as the wits came out and the day wore on. These games were usually played on a Sunday: the better the day, the better the deed.

Melbourne Cup Day was also a favourite occasion for pub cricket matches, Australia being the only country in the world where there is a national public holiday for a horse race. In fact, this particular match which has gone down in history was actually played on Melbourne Cup Day, 1963, in a place called Boraloolla. That day, the crowd got free beer, a free cricket match, a bet on the Cup – and they saw the Eighth Wonder of the World.

There was the usual argument about the most effective way to open a keg without the beer going flat, because most Australians are authorities on opening kegs; and then, after a few grogs to see them go, the captains tossed and the revelry was about to begin.

The umpires were ready to go on to the field, each with a jug of beer in hand to improve his vision so he could give decisions to his own team without fear or favour.

The star of the visiting team, an opening batsman, was also ready; he wore one batting glove (on the wrong hand); one of his pads was white, the other tan; his trousers were navy blue and he wore a tee-shirt labelled BEER IS A FOOD – and a digger's hat. His bat was split and repaired with string dipped in tar.

Two drunks, after a long struggle, had managed to peg down the matting on the asphalt wicket. They then proceeded to put the stumps in, discovered there were only five – and substituted a piece of a branch from a wattle tree with yellow blooms on top of it.

The game was about to proceed when the visiting captain did a slow head count to make sure his team were all present. Only ten men. He double checked. Only ten bloody men.

The captain called on his team to line up. 'There's some bastard missing.'

They lined up rather unsteadily (the bar had been open for two hours). 'We can beat them with a man short,' some smart Aleck said.

'Not without Sammy Smith, one of our opening batsmen, we can't,' the captain said. 'Sammy's definitely not here.'

One of the drunks who had helped put the matting down quipped: 'If Sammy's not here, he must be dead. He wouldn't miss a day of free beer. We'd better send around the hat.'

The visiting captain approached the Boraloolla committee and politely sought a replacement. The Boraloolla mob weren't keen to help out: they'd wagered heavily on the local team.

At last, an old bloke sitting in a cart under a near-by tree, called to the visiting captain: 'Maybe I can help you, mate!'

The captain walked over, a trifle unsteadily, had a look at the old fellow: getting on for eighty, about a dollar's worth of clothes on, corks in his hat and as skinny as a flagpole – would weigh about five stone wringing wet in an army overcoat with housebricks in the pockets.

He'd be useless, the captain decided, and asked, his features suggesting sarcasm and a fondness for beer: 'Fancy yourself as a cricketer, do you, mate?'

'No,' the old bloke replied. 'Never played the game in me life – but my horse is the best opening bat in Queensland.'

'Is he now?' the captain said and, being half pissed and ready for a joke, asked the Boraloolla mob if he could bring in a horse as a replacement for Sammy Smith.

Well, citizens of Boraloolla are all characters (no people there, only characters) so they had a conference around the kegs and agreed: better to have a horse than a ring-in batsman who could play, which they suspected the visitors might be ready to come at.

By this time, the old bloke had unyoked his horse and approached the assembled cricketers.

'Hang on a minute,' he said. 'There's a few conditions attached to this. My horse here is an opening bat, the best in all bloody Queensland, so he will insist on opening the innings and facing the bowling, taking the first over.'

So it was agreed.

'And another thing, he'll want four pads: can't risk him getting injured in a picnic game.'

Well, by this time everybody is laughing their heads off – especially the Boraloolla mob. But the laugh was on the other side of their faces when they tried to scrape up four pads for the horse. The teams had only five pads between them and, as the old bloke was adamant on the horse wearing four of them, the star opening batsman had to surrender his white pad and was left with the tan one – on his wrong leg.

Word went around the town that the Eighth Wonder of the World was about to be seen in Boraloolla – a horse opening the innings in a cricket match on Melbourne Cup Day! So the crowd swelled until six more kegs of beer had to be sent for.

At last, the two openers went to the wicket, amid ribald cheers from the well-oiled throats of the spectators.

The horse took guard – and promptly hit the first ball straight out of the ground for six.

The Boraloolla crowd couldn't believe their eyes, especially when the horse cover drove the second ball for four – cracked the third and fourth balls for six, the fifth for four – and the last ball of the most expensive over ever bowled in Boraloolla for another six.

The star opening batsman faced the second over. He was in form and wanted to get the bowling for himself, so he played down the line until the fifth ball when he called the horse for a single.

But the horse just stood there, leaning on his bat.

When he saw the horse was refusing to run, the star batsman turned and ran back. He nearly got run out.

He scowled at the horse, placed the next ball for an easy single and called again – but the horse didn't move. The star bat went back again and threw himself flat to just scramble home.

He got up, dusted his clothes, went down the wicket to the horse and he said: 'Listen, why didn't you run?'

'Run!' the horse replied. 'If I could run I wouldn't be here playing in a pub cricket match with a mug like you, I'd be down at

Flemington racing in the Melbourne bloody Cup.'

If you don't believe this story you can check the records which show that an eight-year-old gelding made a century against Boraloolla on Melbourne Cup Day, 1963.

From *You Nearly Had Him That Time* by Fred Trueman and Frank Hardy (Stanley Paul)

Alvin Stardust
Minstrel

A couple of years ago, if you had even suggested that I would ever be interested in horses, I would have told you you were completely off your rocker. I was scared stiff of horses. They were just large wild animals that bit and kicked and threw you off. Hence all horsy people were crackpots. All of these things I have since found to be correct. I had only ever been on horseback twice. Once on holiday in Jersey when the horse walked around with me at speeds approaching one mile per week. The next for a photo session in Hyde Park, where I dressed up in a Royal Canadian Mounties outfit that was three sizes too big for me. One of my boots slipped off, the wind blew my hat away and the horse walked over to where it had fallen on the ground and filled it up for me to take home for the roses.

I'm not quite sure why I went for my first lesson, except that I had a feeling that because all our friends seems to be 'into horses', the day would come when someone would say, 'How about us all going riding this afternoon,' and yours truly, not wanting to appear 'wet', would jump on to one of those monsters and gallop off to the nearest General Hospital. Anyway, it appears that my complaint is quite common. In two years I've nearly bought at least five hundred horses, after falling for them all (that could be a slight exaggeration); broken three ribs, done in my right leg, nearly been split in two 'twixt horse and fence, and moved house so that our horse could live 'at home'.

All of which surely makes me a member of the crackpot society.

Willie Carson
A safe bet

At Newmarket they had a lot of daft sayings going round all the time. One of these was 'Have you seen them? The little yellow men?' No one knew what they were; just 'the little yellow men'. One day, 'Bonzo' was riding out with the other lads. They were going round a circular track when someone said to Bonzo, 'Bet you wouldn't ask the guv'nor.' 'Ask him what?' 'About the little yellow men.' Bonzo wasn't all that keen. The guv'nor was a fierce character. He was supposed to be a bit deaf too. Which made him all the more touchy. Before Bonzo could stop him though, the other fella yelled out the guv'nor's christian name. Not at all deaf that day, but twice as irritable by the look of him, the guv'nor spun round immediately. 'What?' he shouted, eyes narrowing, looking for trouble. Too late for Bonzo to withdraw. Besides he was on a dare. He rode over to the guv'nor and said, 'Have you seen them?' 'Seen what?' the guv'nor asked. Bonzo unfortunately started laughing. Behind him the other lads started laughing too. 'Seen what?' demanded the guv'nor. 'What have I seen?' Eventually Bonzo managed to splutter out, 'The little yellow men.' The guv'nor went white. 'Ah, you think you're a comedian do you, my friend? Right. I'll see you later,' and stormed off.

The guv'nor must have had a word with the head lad, because when Bonzo had finished and was quietly crossing the yard trying to make himself scarce for the rest of the day, the head lad suddenly appeared. 'Come 'ere you,' he roared. Bonzo had no chance. 'Right, been trying it on with the guv'nor have you? Fancy yourself as a comedian? Right. I've got a job for you.' 'What's that?' asked Bonzo. The head lad took Bonzo down to the paddock. It was in the days before the stable had an indoor ride and the paddock was laid with a straw ring. The head lad pointed to the straw; he said, 'I want you to come down every afternoon and pick that lot up.'

So, every day, down went Bonzo to the paddock, picked up the heavy sodden straw and put it in heaps for the muck wagon. It took him a week before he was through. And every day the guv'nor's missus used to come down to the paddock with her dog and every day she'd ask, 'Have you seen them yet?'

Robin Gibb
Bee Gee

I do try to ride and I like riding. The funniest story I can think of at the moment happened to me very recently. I made a video for my new record release and while we were filming there was a horse on the set. In the middle of a very romantic passage during which I was leaning on a wall, the horse slowly backed up to it, lifted its tail and shat all over the wall. The shit ran down into a pile on the side and the funny thing was the cameras ignored me, and all four on the set followed it down the wall until it reached the bottom. We all started laughing – obviously the film was held up for a minute or two while we repaired the set!

David Niven

Hollywood legend

I don't believe this is one of the thoughts of Chairman Mao but breaks, good or bad, do come when you least expect them.

I had been doing a fruitless round of the studio casting offices and my last port of call was the United Artists studio on Santa Monica Boulevard. . . . 'Nothing just now, call next week'. . . . So that the sanctity of the studio could be preserved, the entrance to the Casting Office was separated from the main gate by a twelve-foot-high wall of wire netting. I was walking out again when I was hailed from a large limousine on the other side of the cage. 'Hi! how's the golf?' It was the great Douglas Fairbanks himself. He never forgot a face, but he had the greatest difficulty in coming up with a name to match it.

Soon I was on his side of the barricade and setting him right that I was not Bobby Sweeny. He asked what I was doing in Hollywood and I told him. He thought for a moment and said kindly,

'Gee, I hope you make it . . . I'm here with Sylvia at the Beach House and we'd love to see you any time you like. I'd like to take you to play at Bel Air – it's a great course. Come around, I mean it, any time but please don't ask me to help you with your career.'

This was the completely honest expression of a completely honest man and a breath of fresh air in a place where the empty promise was the easy way out.

'Now,' he said, 'I'm going to take a steam – come on in and join me.'

Actually, I would have preferred the offer of a good hot meal but I gratefully tagged along. He greeted everyone he passed with a wide smile and 'Hi! how are you?' It was obvious that he was greatly loved but he was never quite sure who was loving him.

Inside the steam room, I was introduced to various mist-shrouded figures and I found myself sitting stark naked on a marble slab between Darryl Zanuck, the head of Twentieth Century, a new thrusting company which he was just forming, and Joe Schenck, his partner. Opposite sat Charlie Chaplin and Sid Grauman, a famous theatre owner. Present too were Bill Goetz, another associate of Zanuck's, Lew Schreiber, his casting director, Bill Dover, Sam the Barber and Aiden Roark.

The sight and proximity of these great men, combined with the intense heat was almost too much for me but I decided to sit there if it took all night. It might lead to something. They were used to these steam baths. I wasn't. After ten minutes, my lungs felt scalded and my head was spinning.

Fairbanks, above all, loved jokes of any sort, funny jokes, practical jokes, any jokes. He had, of course, caught on that I was practically broke so he couldn't resist saying,

'Oh, Niven, what are you planning this winter? Playing polo or bringing the yacht round?'

'Polo . . . polo,' I croaked and made for the exit. Sam the Barber grabbed me before I fell to the marble floor and put me forcibly into the ice-cold plunge. I was reviving when the others came out of the steam room.

'Doug says you played for the British Army,' said Zanuck.

'Well, I played a bit in Malta,' I mumbled.

'Come and play a few chukkas on Sunday. We'll have a good game.'

'Er . . . my clothes haven't arrived yet, I'm afraid.'

'Aiden here will fix you up.'

Aiden Roark was a ten-goal international. He and his brother Pat both played for Great Britain. Now he was employed by Zanuck in some capacity and organized Zanuck's polo team. A quiet, dark-haired, olive-skinned Irishman, he looked more like a South American. I decided to tell him the truth and in a corner, I explained my limitations.

'Don't worry about it – I'll lend you all the stuff you need. Just play a couple of chukkas – you'll have fun.'

So it was arranged. I was to play polo at the Uplifters Club the following Sunday afternoon with Darryl Zanuck! How many two dollars and fifty cents 'extras' were getting that break?

On the fateful day, Aiden Roark lent me some jodhpurs that were much too tight and drove me to the ground. The first thing that worried me was when I noticed that the stands were full of people. Douglas Fairbanks and the gorgeous Sylvia Ashley were in a box. The second thing which unnerved me was the sight of the other players. Among them were 'Big Boy' Williams, a formidable performer. Elmer Boseke and Cecil Smith, both ten-goal internationals. The final thing, and this nearly completed my disintegration, was the sight of 'Saint George'.

'Saint George' was a white Arab stallion. He bit savagely at everything in sight and at that moment, a groom was struggling to put him into a muzzle.

'You can play Saint George,' said Aiden. 'Play him in the first and fourth chukkas. It's only a pick up game. You play at number one and I'll hit the ball up to you . . . Mark Darryl, he's playing back on the other team . . . wear the red vest.'

The bell went. It was a nightmare. I didn't know who was playing in which position on what team. Those great experts were hitting the ball like a rocket from every direction but during that first chukka, I was far too busy stopping Saint George from leaving the ground altogether to care. When Aiden passed the ball up to me, I made vague flourishes with my stick but quickly needed both hands again to control the brute. It was during one of these mad dashes that Saint George kicked a goal.

Zanuck I tried to cover but generally passed him at high speed without making contact.

At the end of the first chukka, Aiden was laughing so much he could hardly change ponies.

'Come back in for the fourth one . . . you'll find him easier now he's worked some of it off.'

I toyed with the idea of slinking from the ground but I still hoped that I might impress Zanuck and further my movie career, so I waited apprehensively for my next appearance. My riding muscles, suddenly forced into violent action, were now reacting and causing me to shake like a leaf. This did not go unnoticed by Saint George when I mounted him once more for the fourth chukka.

I was determined to make my mark on Zanuck and I stayed as close to him as Saint George would let me. I even hit the ball a couple of times which encouraged me enormously. The experts continued to charge about playing a spectacular game shouting oaths and instructions at each other but Aiden, I suspected, had deliberately stopped sending the ball up to me. It all seemed more peaceful.

Suddenly, 'Big Boy' Williams, renowned as one of the longest hitters in the game, connected from the far end of the ground and the ball sailed over Zanuck's head towards the goal. Zanuck turned fast and galloped off to backhand it away. I chased after him to try and ride him off the line, and if miracles could happen, to score. The two of us were now the focal point of all eyes. People were shouting and clods of earth were flying up into my face from Zanuck's pony's hooves.

Saint George was the faster and we gained inexorably.

As we drew almost level and I was getting into position to bump Zanuck off the line of the ball, Saint George leaned forward and through his muzzle sank his teeth into the seat of Zanuck's breeches. Zanuck roared with alarm and pain and in the ensuing shambles, his pony trod on the ball. It became embedded in the turf. I caught a momentary glimpse of the white mushroom top passing below us and, trying to ignore the embarrassing action at the front end of my steed, I made a vague swipe at it as it fell astern. I missed and my stick passed beneath Zanuck's pony's tail. His mount being extremely sensitive in that area, with a maidenly reaction, clamped its tail to its behind. The head of my stick was thus imprisoned. I was attached by a leather thong around my wrist to the other end of the stick. Saint George had a firm grip on Zanuck's buttocks and our horrible triangle galloped past the stands.

Zanuck was good about it. I was not invited to play polo with him again but he mentions it to this day when I see him.

From *The Moon's a Ballon* by David Niven (Hamish Hamilton, Coronet Books)

David Essex

David Essex

One day Bev Bush, my tour assistant, and I went out for an afternoon on two black stallions. It was a lovely day and both horses were full of life and 'go'. We jumped a hedge into a charming country field, and suddenly both horses went from frisky to berserk. We lost the horses, the seat of Bev's trousers and half of one of my teeth. It transpired that we had jumped the hedge into a paddock of mares on heat. The stallions had a field day.

Russell Grant

Astrologer to the stars

I vaguely remember my grandparents having a horse and charging it round Northolt racecourse. My grandmother was a Sagittarian, and of course Sagittarius rules horses. I've never liked them myself. Not that I object to them as animals; it's just that I've always been frightened they might bite me. They're so human. They know everything you're saying.

I predicted the winner of the Grand National once, 'over the air'. I sort of told the world that Ben Nevis would win, and it did. I was inundated with requests from people wanting lucky numbers, lucky colours, lucky horses, lucky cards, lucky anything to try to win some money. And the spiritual outcome was that I tried to bet on further predictions with horses, as I'd got this one right, and each time I did and it won, I would suffer these problems afterwards. And then I was told by a medium that one should never use one's psychic gifts for material gain, or ill might befall one, and that's why I stopped.

I'd had a 'warning' already. I was due to go to Wolverhampton to predict the result of a football match – a semifinal I think; you know me and sport – we're not that compatible. I went up to Wolverhampton and when I arrived I surveyed the company and the Wolves PR and announced that here I was. They said, 'Oo the 'ell are you?' and I replied that I'd come to do these predictions. 'You're not meant to be 'ere till tomorrow,' they chorused, so I rang my manager who argued with them at some length on the phone, saying there was no mistake: it was meant to be. They, predictably, said it wasn't, and I hung in the balance, waiting to go on the air and predict that Everton would win. Mercifully, with everyone buggered up, they dropped the item. Everton lost 5-nil. But that, if you like, was my warning from the spirit world: 'Right. We're going to let you off this time. But if you'd gone on the air, you would have looked an idiot, wouldn't you?'

Kiri Te Kanawa
Kiwi chorister

I've a passion for horses but I really hate to see them race. I suppose this goes back to when I was a small girl in New Zealand. My parents took me one day to a race meeting. The atmosphere was so exciting, I was really enjoying it all. Then very unfortunately there was an accident, and I saw a poor horse get shot. It upset me terribly. I was sick and cried for a whole week afterwards. Nobody in the house got any sleep, and it was a good two weeks before I managed some kind of a night's sleep myself. Very sad, wasn't it?

Roger Whittaker
More than a balladeer

Over the years I have kept many horses and all of them had their very own, distinctive characters and personalities. Riding and horses are a great passion of mine, yet the most charming of all my equine friends was a donkey.

Monty Gordo – our disreputable ass – came to us when my wife Natalie and I found we had insufficient time to work our two horses and Welsh pony, who was in foal at the time. They needed companionship, and as all three were mares, the obvious solution seemed to be a cheerful, gelded donkey.

We found him in a herd of extremely well-kept donkeys of every description: from immaculate piebalds to positively smooth-coated donks. But, there was Monty, looking like a discarded and very moth-eaten fur coat, with exaggerated ears and a *grin*. We fell for him at once.

Over the six years he was with us, he gave us many headaches, but many, many more laughs. Amongst his quirks were stealing buckets and leaving them at the furthermost point in the fields; playing tag with the barn cats; and he loved music! He was attracted to my studio by the sounds of the musicians and myself rehearsing and I'm sure if he could, he would have sung along with us. However, he spent much of his time frantically searching for the 'other' donkey he could see in the patio window of my studio. One day, he almost found him, and managed to get into the studio while the musicians were at lunch. In no time at all, he demolished microphones, stands, mufflers and a drum kit, although perhaps he was only trying to join in and make his own kind of music.

Above all else, Monty was an escape artist! Once, during haymaking, we had to move all the animals to a field further away. The very first time Natalie and I took the mares out for exercise, we had gone no further than a mile, when a braying and kicking Monty joined us. Repeatedly, I returned him to his field, checking and double-checking the fencing and sliding rails that formed the gate, the lowest of which was just *eighteen* inches from the ground. There was absolutely no way he could jump the top rail; there was no way he could open the gate, which was bolted at all times. But, somehow, he was managing to escape.

So one morning, in desperation, I laid a trap for him. While Natalie took the horses on their daily exercise, I hid in the hedge nearby that afforded me a good view of Monty's paddock. As soon as the horses disappeared from sight, Monty put his head over the rails, looked left and right to see if the coast was clear and no one was watching, then carefully lowered himself on to his knees. He then lay as flat as he possibly could and wriggled inch by inch *under* the bottom rail. As soon as he was clear of the barrier, he leapt to his feet with a look of unmitigated glee, shook himself all over and trotted off down the road. At that moment, I jumped from my hiding place, in front of him.

Monty's expression changed immediately to that of a small boy who had been caught scrumping. He sulked – a feat at which he was expert – for a good week after we fixed a bar only nine inches off the ground with a challenge to him to try and limbo under! He never did, but I'm sure he made a very good attempt.

Kevin Keegan

Sporting hero

Mike Channon, who is a great friend of mine, being a great footballer, had a mare. And it was running in a race called the Brown Jack Stakes. A quarter partner share in the horse with him was a lad called Brian O'Neal, who was also a footballer. So we went down to watch the four quarters of this horse actually run.

The trainer was a man called Bill Wightman (no relation), who's a real gentleman. Now, it was Ascot, and it was a lovely day, and in the parade ring before the race they stood there with the horse, talking to the trainer and waiting for the jockey to turn up. It was Willie Carson. So first of all Bill Wightman said, 'Now, listen, Willie, if the horse wants to go out in front and make the running, then I don't see any reason why you should hold her back, because she's a good strong mare and she's quite happy to make the pace.' And then Mickey, trying to keep up with the conversation, put in, 'Yes, Willie, don't try to hold her back because she tends to be better when she's front running; she's happier that way.' Brian O'Neal, who's a very quiet lad, stood at the back, listening to all this. He had quite a big bet on the horse so, at the end, just as Willie was mounting up, he came over and looked the jockey in the eye. 'See all those horses, Willie?' he said, casting technicalities aside. 'They're bloody Indians and you're a cowboy. You just keep well in front and don't let them catch you.'

Lucinda Green
Queen of eventing

David and I were competing in our first international event together since we were married, in the Irish championships last spring. During the briefing, which is a rather serious affair where they tell us this, that and the other about the rules, the organizer stood up and announced that the course was measured to however many metres it was: 'We've put a half-way marker in where the half-way mark is. But to be sure,' he added sternly, 'we think the second half is longer than the first.'

Lionel Blair
Prince of dance

When Janet Scott was married to Jacky Ray, they had a big house in the country, and invited me down for a weekend. I'd never been on a horse before but when I got on one I found I was quite good. They made me ride all day. I was enjoying it, but then they made me do a jump which nearly crippled me. I mean I can't tell you. They said a little jump.

I remember it so well: going to bed and thinking, 'Ooh, golly that hurts!' And I looked in the mirror and there was this bruising at the bottom of my spine and down my thighs. Black and blue. Now I really mean black and blue. I had to sleep on my tummy all night, I couldn't move. No dance routine, ever, has hurt me as much as that ride.

Little jump indeed! Jacky had held the reins and said, 'Go on, try it.' And I'll never forget it, it brought tears to my eyes.

Ted Edgar
Eloquent equestrian

Well, I've got bloody hundreds of bloody stories, but 'ere's a quick one. We went to a show the other day and we've got a driver there who's Irish. Seven or eight 'orses on the lorry and we had to take 'em off the lorry to push the lorry out of a quagmire to get it started. We're pushing the lorry out and Ted Campion says to the Irish driver, 'Now once you f...ing get going, don't you stop till you get to f...ing Munich.' Well, this lad f...ed off down the road five miles and they had to send a car to get him back. He said, 'Well, you told me not to stop till I got to Munich.' It's the truth I tell you. Eddie Macken was going crazy. He said, 'For f... sake! We'll never live this down.' And Campion said, 'Ooh, for f... sake get him out of the driving seat. Fancy going without the horses.'

Stewart Granger
Screen idol

I remember when I went for my first part as a cowboy. Of course I was supposed to be able to ride. But of course I lied. So I hastily took some riding lessons. Well, I turned up for lesson one, togged up in new riding boots, breeches, hat and jacket, and with great difficulty managed to mount up. The rest of the pupils in the lesson consisted of a group of very giggly young girls, all of whom could ride very well.

We set off on a hack, and it wasn't long before all that jogging up and down made me want to pee. Of course there was no way that I could get off the horse, because I would never be able to get back on again. I decided to try to wait until the end of the lesson. But the jogging up and down carried on and soon I was in pain. Suddenly I had an idea. I slowed the horse down, and let the girls go on ahead. When they were out of sight I stood up in the saddle and began to relieve myself. Unfortunately the horse took fright and bolted. I was so frightened. I couldn't stop peeing and was desperately trying to hang on. Eventually the horse slowed down, and I was able to get myself together. I found that I had soaked my new jodhpurs and filled my boots. The girls soon reappeared and the giggles started. The situation was pretty obvious to them. I didn't know where to put myself. I was so embarrassed. Even now when I think back to it, I start to blush.

Hugh McIlvanney
The oracle of sport

Oh I have been to Ludlow Fair
And left my necktie God knows where

Mr A. E. Housman should have gone to Ludlow races, and tried holding on to his shirt. The poet's ashes, resting in a nearby churchyard, may have stirred gently in sympathy around 3 o'clock on Wednesday afternoon as Marungu, backed to 5–2 on in a three-horse steeplechase, came home a weary, one-paced second.

An hour before, an 11-year-old called The Spaniard also asked to beat two opponents, had been made 11–4 on to do the job. He went under by a short head to Jimmy Bourke on Miss Dorothy Squires' Esban and even that lady's traditional reception of her heroes, which involves scattering kisses like moistened buckshot, could not drown the groaning of the wounded.

By the time Marungu's failure had taken its toll, the misty Shropshire air was loud with talk of atrocities and strong men were wondering if the Geneva Convention could be applied to National Hunt racing. Some of the worst sufferers were battle-toughened punters from the urban Midlands. At an ordinary flat race meeting the invisible handcuffs forged by long experience would have kept them from laying such dubious odds – odds that were made even less attractive by the inroads of betting tax. But here in the friendly and historic countryside, under a tiny stand with the pillared and fretted façade of a Victorian railway station, they succumbed to the rustic charm of it all.

For a few lightheaded moments they seemed to imagine that they were at one of those point-to-points where odds-on favourites are safe from practically all hazards short of a well-aimed hand grenade. So they went over the top and were mowed down while the more venerable of the local farmers, rosy and whiskered and dateless, watched them with the ambivalent sympathy a fox might give to a lemming.

On past form, I should have been with the lemmings, but this day was different. I had not gone to Ludlow as a mug. I had gone as an owner. Well, as a surrogate owner, second class. To come clean, two friends of mine own a hurdler called Overall and, since one of them was in the Canaries and the other was showing a moving sense of duty by staying at his desk in the *Daily Express*, I was elected travelling representative.

Looking at Ludlow on the map, one had the impression that the trip would take about three hours in a Boeing 747. But the prospect was irresistible. Apart from all its other attractions this sortie would keep me away from some of the predictable temptations of my first week back in sportswriting, such as running off at the mouth and the ballpoint about Brian Clough, that alternately admirable and exasperating man whose dramas have become slightly less riveting than the music of Syncopating Sandy, the marathon piano player.

Anyway, I reflected during the drive up through the West Country, through those stone-built villages that make grey seem the warmest colour in the world, the Flat was ending this weekend. National Hunt racing was about to resume its winter monopoly, to demonstrate again its popularity and confirm that it holds an important place among the sporting pleasures of the nation.

Before we reached Worcester I was musing on all the statistics that made a journey to Ludlow on an overcast Wednesday in October an essential contribution to any serious analysis of leisure activities in the early seventies. Had not the man at William Hill's assured me that their volume of betting, which once diminished spectacularly at the close of the Flat, is now reduced by a mere 15 or 20 per cent when the jumpers take over? Had not the Racing Information Bureau reported that attendances at National Hunt meetings in 1972 numbered 1,419,971, despite the competition of 16,000 betting shops and endless coverage of the sport on television? Yes, they had.

But by the time we pulled into Ludlow racecourse, I had owned up. My presence in Shropshire had nothing to do with facts and figures or the rising status of National Hunt racing. I had been towed there by a fantasy. Ever since I learned to read a form line (surely one of the vital uses of literacy that Richard Hoggart

43

neglected) I have fantasized privately about being an owner. Now, for a day, I had a licence to play the game in public. Most of my daydreams have had Epsom as their setting, with Lester and my champion three-year-old treating the Derby field as a shark might treat a shoal of mackerel.

Overall is a four-year-old gelding and he was running in a novice hurdle worth £204 to the winner, but I was happy enough to carry his banner. Wearing my owner's badge like a breastplate, I was testing the ground before I was halfway out of the car. Overall doesn't like the firm and I was relieved to find my heel sinking in an inch or so. 'This will do us,' I said professionally.

'Yes,' said my companion, 'if they run the race through the car park he's a good thing.'

I gave him a brief glare and went in search of Richard Smith, who was to ride for me, I mean us or even them. Smith, a farmer's son who was champion amateur rider before he started bringing in winners for money, is thin-faced and intense and not inclined to be garrulous. The ground was a shade firmish, he said, but it wouldn't be a problem. I began to flex my punting hand as I went to meet Jenny Kennard, the wife of Overall's trainer. Les Kennard had urgent business at the Newmarket Sales and had delegated Jenny to bring the horse up from Taunton.

She turned out to be a pleasant, lively lady with much of the West Country practicality and horse sense that have made her husband a telling force around the circuit. Still wearing her smart mauve coat and white fur hat, she moved in briskly to prepare Overall for his work. The little, light-framed horse stood with the dignity of a bullfighter being dressed for the ring while the saddle was strapped on him and the girths were tightened.

He looked reserved, but no more humble than he had a right to be after winning the second of his two previous hurdle races by 12 lengths, at Wincanton. He is no scrubber and Mrs Kennard agreed that he should be able to give weight and a beating to the 18 hurdlers against him. She gave his face a last wipe with a wet sponge, then squeezed it in his mouth, saying with a laugh: 'A drop of gin and tonic before you go.'

I telephoned my friend in Fleet Street with the reassurance and we made our concerted assault on the enemy. We took a little 2–1, a little 15–8 and quite a lot of 7–4 and left the masses with the evens.

44

I am inclined to describe every stride of the two miles, one furlong and 20 yards of the race, but we triumphant owners must preserve a sense of modesty. It is enough to say that when Overall came to the line Richard Smith was holding enough leather to make a pair of training gloves for Muhammad Ali, and it would have taken the Jodrell Bank telescope to find the rest of the field.

Mrs Kennard, Mrs Smith and the rest of us who could be considered what Richard Baerlein loves to call 'the connections', swilled a little champagne, as connections do, and set off happily for home. On the way I had to be forcibly restrained from stopping to make phone calls to Vincent O'Brien and John Mulcahy. I would like to make them aware that if they need someone to lead in Apalachee when the colt wins next year's Guineas and Derby, I am their man.

'The Shropshire Nag', reprinted from *The Observer*

Groucho Marx
A Marx brother

Several years ago, testosterone hit the front pages. This was a magic serum from Vienna which had been extracted from some part of a horse. Which part, I do not care to discuss publicly, but I'll tell you this – if it wasn't for that part there wouldn't be any young horses today.

The theory was that if you took twelve shots over a period of three months, you would once again regain the vigour and vitality of a four-year-old stallion. For a man with low blood pressure and occasional suicidal tendencies, this seemed like a short cut to the legendary fountain of youth and all that it implied. An hour after reading this glowing article, I was in the doctor's office getting my first injection. Each morning on arising I looked hopefully in the mirror for my vanished youth. I saw many things in that glass. I saw a decrepit face bordering on degeneracy, a sagging chin, and enough decay to fill fifteen or twenty teeth, but nowhere did I see anything that resembled what I had hoped for.

After the twelfth stab with the doctor's magic bullet I came to the reluctant conclusion that this, too, was a snare and a delusion, that the doctor was a dirty crook and that the happy vista I had visualized was a sexual mirage that could never be reached unless there was something to this nonsense about reincarnation.

Some months later, while on my way to the poorhouse, I ran into this charlatan (who was on his way to the bank) and who, by that time, had extracted two hundred and forty hard dollars from my pants and tucked them into his.

'Groucho!' he exclaimed, stepping back a few feet to survey me. 'No, it can't be Groucho! Are you the same man who came to see me three months ago, a total wreck? Why you don't look a day over thirty! Are you sure you're not Tony Curtis?' 'Of course I'm sure,' I snapped. 'I'm Groucho Marx and if you're still not convinced I'll drive home and get my driver's licence and show it to you.'

He smiled falsely, but doggedly continued, 'I presume the testosterone shots were effective, otherwise you would have been back to visit me. You look like a new man. How do you feel?' he asked, stroking the pocket with my money in it. 'I feel lousy,' I answered. 'Hmmmmm,' he mumbled as he pulled his left ear lobe reflectively. 'Are you telling me that the injections didn't work?' 'Oh, the injections worked fine, Doc, but the medicine wasn't worth a damn.' 'Come now,' he insisted, 'didn't the testosterone do anything for you at all?'

'Well, yes it did,' I admitted. 'Yesterday I was out at Santa Anita and I did the mile in two minutes and ten seconds!'

Reprinted with the permission of the publisher, Bernard Geis Associates, from *Memoirs of a Mangy Lover* by Groucho Marx. © 1963 by Groucho Marx

Margaret Thatcher
First lady

Q. 'Why is a new MP like a famished horse?'
A. 'Because they're both hungry for a pair/pear and daren't disobey a Whip.'

The PM has been fond of the poetry of Rudyard Kipling ever since she was a little girl, especially lines like the following:

'Four things greater than all things are:
Women and Horses and Power and War.'

Rula Lenska
Flame-haired star

One day I was at a shoot and the film called for some people on horseback and carriages, and the biggest most handsome horse there was this enormous Shire horse. So I went over to say hello and it took a liking to me and followed me. Then unfortunately it stood on my foot. Which was bad enough, but there was worse to come. Nobody could get it off!

Dennis Waterman

Actor and recording artist

We were into an episode of 'Minder' which involved me guarding this thoroughbred racehorse. Come night time, it was decided that the best way to keep an eye on this horse was for me to sleep in the stall with it. So this bloody funny scriptwriter decided that the horse should make a loud fart just as I was settling down to sleep. I was to act as if the horse had 'passed wind' and they would dub on the sound later. But when it came to the take, the horse farted on cue, and because we all fell about laughing at this, we had to take it again. Blow me if he didn't give a repeat performance, and he farted to order from then on till the end of the shooting. Remarkable, eh!

David Bailey
King of the camera

When asked what he thought about horses, David replied that he
didn't think about them. But if he did it was only when the cart was
before the horse.

Alan Smith
Horseback writer

When the People's Republic of China was admitted to membership during the General Assembly of the International Equestrian Federation in Geneva in December 1982, their delegate, instead of merely standing, thanking the Bureau of the Federation and sitting down again, as is the custom, chose the occasion to make a political speech, pointing out what flags and anthems China-Taipei, already members of the IEF, would be allowed to fly and play under a recent ruling by the International Olympic Committee.

Prince Philip, President of the IEF, listened with rapidly diminishing patience for about a minute and a half and then interrupted to say, 'I don't think that's relevant. As you know the IEF has no interest in anthems or flags. If any of you want, you can play Colonel Bogey, and fly a pair of knickers.'

Robin Cousins
Ice-man

One day I was asked by Lord March to go down to the New Forest area to judge a competition which was organized in conjunction with the British Equestrian Association. I was a bit worried because I don't know that much about horses, but Lord March told me that it would all become clear when I got there.

The event went on and there was a special section where a set of horses came out and did a dressage exhibition, choreographed to music. I couldn't believe the precision and obvious amount of concentrated training that had gone into it. In fact, I was so impressed that I ended up taking notes for tips!

Terry Biddlecombe
Champion hedge hopper

It is difficult to define my feelings before my first Grand National. The only person who had told me anything about Liverpool was Michael Scudamore. He had a great record in the National in which he rode for sixteen consecutive years, finishing second in 1952 on Legal Joy, third on Irish Lizard in 1954 and winning on Oxo in 1959.

I remember that the night before the 1960 race we had a light dinner; then everybody else went out and I was the little boy who was left alone in the hotel. I lay in bed, half-asleep, thinking about what I was going to do in the race – as I was to do before other Grand Nationals. I was there, going to the last with no chance, wishing that the horses in front would all fall and I would win the race! Then, I'd been brought down and remounted, and at that point in my fantasies even to have been second would have been great. These things raced through my mind all night, and I woke up in the morning feeling ghastly.

The routine that followed was fairly predictable with all the ensuing Grand Nationals in which I rode. Schooling on the track in the early morning at Liverpool has never ceased to exhilarate me. Even in my later days when I had no ride in the race I would go and watch the horses work. There is a bit of dew on the grass; the stands are empty; the air is fresh and clean and there are very few people around.

After schooling I would nip into the weighing room to see what weight I was and then knew how much breakfast I could have or, better still, drink half a bottle of champagne in the baths while shedding a few pounds. Most of us stayed at Southport, especially those who were wasting, and after breakfast we would go into the Turkish baths where we would fool around a bit, pretending to argue as to who was to buy the first bottle. This helped everyone to forget the bad dreams of the night before. There would be at least ten or twelve jockeys in there who really had to get the weight off. If you did not have to lose any yourself, you still went in to help the others and share the champagne.

There was one little steam room at Southport about as big as an old-fashioned wooden-seated lavatory, with a whistling draught coming in under the door which made your feet cold and stopped you sweating. In my day, we had an old masseur who never stopped running and bustling about like a busy old lady, pushing bowls of hot water under the door for you to put your feet into and thereby keeping your body temperature high.

When you went from the steam room into the hot room it always seemed that you were not losing weight as the perspiration dried on your skin as soon as it appeared. This sometimes made you panic and go for a swim, only to find that your body had re-absorbed water, so it was back to the hot room again.

The masseur would go out at about 9.30 in the morning and bring back some champagne or fresh orange juice, which refreshed everybody. Then we would all have to leave by 11 o'clock because we had to check out of our hotels before noon on the morning of the National. These sweating sessions were enormous fun, talking, laughing and generally relaxing before the big race.

After leaving the baths we would go to the course and into the weighing room. I usually rode in a hurdle race before the National as a warm-up. Michael Scudamore disapproved of this because he felt that the risk of injury before the big race was too great.

Then came the National itself. The weighing room was so quiet. There were no jokes then, and the only character in my day who could be lighthearted was Johnny Lehane, and I suspect that he had had a few more brandies than the rest of us. It was impossible to get into the lavatory because it was full of jockeys. I have never seen so many trying to have a last 'go' – if you had held a tablespoon under them they could not have filled it. The weighing room was filled with tension. Some jockeys would light a cigarette, just before being called out, and then immediately extinguish it. Others did not speak. Lord Sefton would come in and deliver a little speech, asking us to go steadily at the first. I suppose we took a bit of notice, especially in later years after the great pile-up of 1967. When you walked out into the paddock and got a leg up it was suddenly like any other race. There was the thrill of the parade, going to post, and lining up, trying to edge into your chosen place, but I think I speak for everyone when I say that my own thoughts then were only that I had a job to do. There were tens of thousands of people watching but, apart from hoping that they had put their money in the right place, I used to go out and enjoy myself.

My first ride in the National on Aliform was very exciting. I had just turned professional, I was riding an old favourite and he jumped those Liverpool fences perfectly. I asked Michael Scudamore how to recognize Becher's Brook and he said, 'When you come to the straw path, keep kicking.' I crossed the straw path the first time round and Aliform cleared Becher's like a bird. It was a great feeling. Before this, just to make sure that I knew where the fence was, I had asked 'Taffy' Jenkins during the race to tell me when we were approaching it. We had just crossed the straw path at the time and his reply was, 'It's the fence after this one.' 'This one' was Becher's itself and as we landed I shouted at him, 'We've just jumped it, you fool!' Taffy never knew where Becher's was and he was the one man who should as he had worn out more pairs of boots walking back from it than most of us.

The second time round my horse was tiring. I started kicking after crossing the famous straw path, but he landed on his head at Becher's and my first Grand National was over. As I lay on the grass, slightly winded and feeling a bit choked at falling, who should be there but Scudamore, who had fallen at the fence the first time round and had waited there to watch me. He gave me an almighty kick in the ribs and said, 'Come on, get up, you're not hurt.'

I could have murdered him.

I was to get my own back later on at Newton Abbot when he fell at the last fence on a horse called Archavon. I was the spectator then and seized my chance. I gave Michael a kick which he has since said was harder than any horse could have dealt him and said, 'Get up, you silly bugger, you are all right,' and he had to laugh.

From *Winner's Disclosure* by Terry Biddlecombe (Stanley Paul)

Ricardo Montalban
Actor and Mexican

(Talking about *Across the Wide Missouri* with Clark Gable)

I had prepared for my role. I was playing a Blackfoot warrior, and I studied the tribe's language and customs with an authority, Nippo Strongheart. I exercised and rode horseback so I could convincingly portray an Indian brave. I arrived early at the location near Durango and watched the filming, swam in the motel pool, and enjoyed the brisk, clean atmosphere of the Rockies. As I stood on the hill overlooking the location, I decided it was time to get acquainted with the horse I was to ride in the movie. Two days later my role would begin, and I wanted to be sure that the horse and I would be comfortable together.

He was a magnificent animal, a pinto that pranced around the corral full of raw energy. The Colorado air seemed to have envigorated him, too; also the fresh mountain grass. The pinto had been shipped from Los Angeles, and hadn't been ridden in a couple of weeks; he was feeling bright and frisky.

I had to ride him Indian-style in the movie, and I decided to give it a tryout. No saddle. Not even a halter, only a piece of rope tied around his jaw. I liked the idea of giving horse and rider an authentic, exciting, primitive look. But first I'd better see if I could control the pinto with only a piece of rope. I catapulted onto his back.

The pinto responded immediately, instinctively, reacting as if he had never had a rider on his back. Not leaping like a bronco, but prancing with total independence. 'Time to let him know who's the boss, Ricardo,' I instructed myself.

I tightened the rein. I realized I would have to establish my control or he would never perform before the camera. At first I tried to walk him. Impossible. He was simply not inclined to walk. I tried a gentle gallop, but it didn't work.

'Okay, pardner, if you want to run, we'll run,' I said, and I opened him up. The pinto went racing across the hill, and I felt the exhilaration of a roller coaster at an amusement park. But unlike in a roller coaster, I felt in control. I held tightly to the rein, and I let him know who was boss. I guided him down the hill and then turned him gently around, so he had to climb the incline. This would tire him, I realized, and bring him under better control. Now he was beginning to gentle, to realize the fatigue that came with exertion in the mile-high atmosphere. He slowed, and I let him walk. Then I urged a gallop, and walked him again. He became more responsive. Now he welcomed the chance to abandon the chase.

I rode him to the top of the hill, where sprouts of grass were pushing through the earth. He seemed exhausted, and I welcomed the chance to rest myself. I turned sideways on the horse, loosening the rope so he could graze. With my left leg dangling, I gazed idly down at the film company in the meadow.

BOOM!

All of a sudden a prop cannon on the film location below exploded with a noise that ricocheted off the mountain walls. I was startled, the pinto was terrified. He started racing down the hill. He was not bucking, but he kicked up his legs as he raced along, and it was impossible for me to regain a riding position. All I could do was hold on as well as possible and hope that the frightened horse would run out of steam.

But he didn't. He kept hurtling down the slope faster and faster, and the ride was getting bouncier. I was not frightened, because I had been thrown from horses dozens of times as a boy on ranches in Mexico. And the hill was covered with soft tufted grass that would make the landing not too painful.

No, I perceived, it wasn't all grass. A hundred feet ahead I could see a boulder about a foot high, perfectly round. Just as a boy on a bicycle says, 'I mustn't hit that tree,' and then hits it, I found myself thinking, 'I mustn't hit that rock.' At that moment the pinto stopped abruptly. I somersaulted through the air and fell on my back. On the rock.

I lay stunned. My breath had left me, and when I tried to rise I found my legs wouldn't move. I fell back, my eyes staring at the brilliant Colorado sky.

The picture finished, and I returned to Los Angeles for more medical examinations. No damage could be found, yet the pain continued and my left leg remained difficult to move. I was advised to exercise, then the leg would return to normal and the pain would disappear. It never has. I went to gyms and exercised with weights, and the leg never improved. And pain has been my constant companion since that clear Colorado day in 1950.

From *Reflections* by Ricardo Montalban (Doubleday, 1980)

Liza Goddard
Actress, wife and mother

When Liza was a young girl, she was teaching at 'Mrs Carter's' in Frensham Pond during her school holidays. One day Mrs C told her to take this client, a Mr Twee (honest) and give him a lesson. She warned that although he was in his thirties, he was extremely nervous and that she was only to allow him in the field. So she led him very quietly and carefully down there. She let go of the rein and turned round to close the gate. The horse took off around the field and cleared all the jumps that were set up and then walked back over to Liza. Mr Twee was shaking and said, 'Gosh. I didn't think I'd get on to jumping on my first lesson.' Liza just swallowed and said, 'Oh well, very good.'

60

Alan Ayckbourn
Literary light

I have never been near a horse in my life. Sorry!

Well, when I was six, I went to a point-to-point and a horse ran into the fence with a ghastly crunch. A nice kindly looking middle-aged vet came across, apparently to pat the poor beast on the head, and promptly shot it.

I've stuck to cows ever since.

Patrick Moore

Astronomer to the stars

I like horses very much but I think you could say my equine ignorance is complete.

I do like horses. They are pleasant, friendly animals. I do *not* like horsy people; one immediately becomes involved with individuals who enjoy fox-hunting and stag-hunting, which I regard with the deepest contempt. How any decent person can find pleasure in killing, particularly in a disgusting way, is something which defeats me. Therefore I have never had a great deal to do with horses – though on one occasion I did try to ride one.

It was at the beginning of the war – 1940, when I was in Canada learning how to fly. One weekend on short leave, I and several others went to stay with friends in Oakville, which is near Toronto. They had a horse (or several horses) and I was persuaded to try to ride one. I am not naturally agile – it has been said that I give every impression of having been somewhat hastily constructed – and it was with difficulty and assistance that I finally got on to the creature's back. The effect was electric. The horse turned its head round, stared at me, and made what I can only describe as a disapproving noise. I immediately fell off on the other side of the horse. And that was the end of my riding career. Henceforth I confine my riding activities strictly to a bicycle.

Robin Knox-Johnston
Lone sailor

I was taught to ride at the age of four, but you can't do much riding at sea so I have not done very much since. On this particular occasion I had just heard that I had passed my Masters Certificate which entitles you to be a captain on a ship. I heard the news on a Friday and on the Saturday a friend and I went to the pub to celebrate. In the afternoon we went out for a walk. There were four horses in one field and, full of confidence no doubt alcohol induced, I leapt on the back of one of them to prove I could still ride. I stayed on for approximately twelve seconds, for ten of which the horse didn't move. For the last two it moved very rapidly and I then left it describing a graceful arc to the ground. A Red Arrow-type plane chose this moment to fly over upside down and the thought went through my mind, 'This chap can fly high'; I half expected someone on a cloud to come and give me harp lessons. Then I became aware of a rather pungent smell – my head was a hair's breadth from a cow pat and that brought me back to earth with a bang. It rather put me off riding again.

David Foster
Waldorf chef

I had a *commis* chef working for me once who was prone to disappear from the kitchens, but always turned up just in time for his tasks. One day I caught him at the telephone laying bets with the local bookie, and it came out in the conversation afterwards that this chef liked a flutter on the horses. Not being a gambler myself I couldn't understand why he chanced his earnings so regularly. Then one day he invited me to the races at Newbury. He told me that once I'd smelled the turf and sensed the atmosphere there and perhaps even had a winner or two, I'd be hooked for life.

It was a beautiful day. We wined and dined well and strolled down to lay on our bets. I was told that we'd have to spot our horses in the paddock to get their form. My *commis* chef was four sheets to the wind by this time, from all the champagne, and while we were in the paddock a very pretty young mare strolled by. 'Hallo my lovely,' he said. 'I recognize the pace but I can't remember the mane.'

Toyah
Singing and wrestling phenomenon

When somebody asks you to name your secret fantasy and you tell them it is to ride a white horse through a large department store, you hardly believe it will ever come true. But ... mine did! Courtesy of TV-am, the commercial breakfast television station.

They arranged for my dream to become reality and fixed it for me to ride a white charger through Liberty's, the Regent Street store ... and they duly filmed the occasion for one of their programmes.

It was one of the most frightening experiences of my life! There was hardly any room in the store for the horse to manoeuvre around the counters, and I was very apprehensive that the horse might rear when faced with a bank of television cameras and press photographers. But he was as good as gold and very well behaved.

Amid all the confusion and chaos, however, there was a very light-hearted moment. Following behind the horse on his canter, was a little man with a dustpan and brush ... just in case.

It was a great opportunity for me, too, to renew an old friendship with the horse, who was called 'Messenger'. The last time I rode him was for filming the promotional video for my record 'Brave New World'. Only on that occasion, we rode around ... Battersea Power Station.

Michael Parkinson
Televisual phenomenon

When I first went to Royal Ascot it was only the third time that I
had ever attended a race meeting. The first occasion was a Pit-
man's Derby when the winner of the 3.30 shot home like a stuck pig
after having a tie-pin inserted in its backside by a jockey who was
most certainly not a friend of the Duke of Norfolk.

My second visit to a racecourse was altogether more auspicious.
I was working on a newspaper in Doncaster and was sent to the
racecourse to write the gossipy stuff. I fulfilled my commitment an
hour before the first race, retired to the bar and emerged five hours
later blind as a mole and twice as ignorant about the sport of
kings.

So it was with a degree of pessimism that I drove to Ascot. I
parked the car and was immediately approached by an obsequious
gentleman selling tips. He told me I had a lucky face and sold me
two tips for £1. My wife, who is the only person in the world who
knows less about horse racing than myself, said I wanted my brains
tested and that the only way to pick a winner was to back the best-
looking jockey wearing the nicest colour scheme.

Together in blissful ignorance we entered the racecourse and
made for the paddock, because my wife reckoned that her theory on
backing horses could only work if she were close enough to the jockey
to see the colour of his eyes.

The first parade of horses only confirmed what I had always
believed, that when you have seen one racehorse you've seen the
lot. My wife did not share my point of view. 'That jockey there has
a nice smile,' she said. 'What price is he?' I said with a sneer. 'He's
got blue eyes and they match his shirt,' she said in that infuriating
way that women have. 'Put your money where your mouth is
woman,' I said. She put ten bob each way on Sky Rocket because
she liked the look of the jockey. I put my money on the horse my

tipster friend had given me and then put a quid on Sky Rocket just in case.

Before the 'off' I met a friend of mine supposedly versed in the ways of racing animals. When I told him what we had backed he gave us a sympathetic look and bought us a drink. He then explained that the last competition Sky Rocket had won was a ploughing contest and that bookmakers were delighted with suckers like us. My wife remained adamant about the jockey's eyes and I pretended I wasn't with her.

Ten minutes later Sky Rocket had won, the Parkinsons were £50 better off than when they arrived at Ascot and I was telling my friend about the last time I interviewed Lester.

Thus enriched I began to soak in the Ascot scene. The first thing you realize is that we British have a unique ability to savour our pleasures painfully. This masochism is obvious in the clothes people wear. The men, as uniform as a regiment of penguins in frock-coats and toppers, look as uncomfortable as you might expect considering that 50 per cent were wearing someone else's suit.

But their discomfort is nothing compared to that enjoyed by the women who wear tall hats in high winds and flimsy dresses in temperatures guaranteed to give an Eskimo a headcold. This being the case it is little wonder that the crowd at Ascot is the quietest sporting assembly I have ever come across. It is difficult to abandon oneself to sporting pleasure when one is covered with goose pimples as big as golf balls.

The crowd around the paddock suffered in silence as the horses paraded by in that prissy, high-stepping way that thoroughbreds have. Only occasionally was the odd thought put into words.

I stood behind a couple who were obvious contenders for the title of Mr & Mrs Ascot of the year. He in morning dress and carrying a gold-topped cane, she in a tiny wispy mini and a hat the size of a cartwheel. After careful and silent contemplation of the field she turned to her partner and said: 'Do you know what darling?' He leant towards her full of expectation, and so did I, hoping to glean some secret tip. 'What darling?' he said. She turned to him with a radiant smile: 'There's a bloody great draught blowing right up my skirt,' she said sweetly. 'Really,' he said, as if she had told him something of great fascination. 'Yes, she said. 'My bum is freezing.' 'My word,' he said and they both resumed their rapt observation of the horses.

By this time the fame of my wife as a tipster had spread far and wide. We were being approached by people to see what we fancied. But as quickly as she had discovered her secret gift so it disappeared. The blue-eyed jockey in the 4.55 with the nice yellow shirt turned out to be the best-looking loser of the day. My wife blamed the champagne which had been flowing like tap-water ever since our win. Like most women she firmly believes that beginners' luck is feminine intuition. None the less it was with cash in hand that we sat and watched the crowds disperse.

I was contemplating the beauty of the scene when I was approached by a gentleman carrying a large and exceedingly boring photograph of a line of ancient taxis. The caption read: 'Ascot 1920'. He sold it to my friend for five pounds. After he had departed I asked the purchaser why anyone would pay five pounds for a photograph of a line of taxis. 'Because it is rare,' he said, fondly studying his purchase. 'Rare?' I asked. 'How many people do you know who have a photograph of a line of taxis?' he said. I was still considering his devastating logic as I drove home.

The more I thought about it, the more it seemed to be the perfect ending to a day at Royal Ascot. It summed up that quality I most admire in my fellow-countrymen, the capacity for doing absurd things in the most dignified manner. I'd forgotten how good at it we were until I went to Ascot.

From *Sporting Fever* by Michael Parkinson (Stanley Paul)

Alan Jones
Digger and racer

When I won the 1980 French Grand Prix I went up on the rostrum after having finished the race. There was a horse up there with a little sign over it saying 'OK Corral'. I didn't quite know why the horse was there, but after just having won a 200-mile grand prix you don't really care.

They kept on saying, 'Hop on the horse, hop on the horse,' and I was saying, 'Look I don't want to hop on the bloody horse, forget it!' I finally got off the rostrum and did my lap of honour in an open car. Then I'm home having a shower and a cold beer when there's a knock at the door, and there's this guy holding the bloody horse again. I say to the bloke, 'What is it with you people? What's going on with this horse?' He tells me, 'In actual fact you won the horse, Mr Jones.' So here I am down in the south of France, an Australian living in England, having just been presented with a horse.

I've got a farm in Australia and I've also got a four-year-old bay. So the horse went from Marseilles to Holland (because it was owned by the Benbar brothers who own amusement arcades) and from Holland to England. It had its blood tests in England, and then it flew out to Australia, as a thoroughbred companion, to Sydney, and then it was road-transported from Sydney to my farm about 500 miles away. So now this little Shetland pony, from starting out life giving kids rides around the 'OK Corral' in the south of France has now been completely and utterly spoilt rotten in his own little paddock sixty miles northeast of Melbourne, Australia right around the other side of the world. It cost me more than Farlett (a very famous Australian racehorse) to ship it around there. But it's a walking trophy and it has become part of the family.

* * *

Another time I got thrown off a horse and broke my hip. And so if I've had one person, I've had about 500 say, 'Jonesy can't even handle one horsepower now; he used to be able to handle 500-odd.'

Joan Bader
Widow of Sir Douglas Bader

Joan's work as an instructor for the Riding for the Disabled Association is, for the most part, centred now on the Royal Mews at Buckingham Palace or, as Douglas would have it, 'opposite the Girl Guides' shop in Buckingham Palace Road'. Although all ages are catered for, her concern is primarily with the young.

The children, who range from five to six upwards, and who are brought to the Mews by minibus once a week for their riding lessons, are drawn from special schools in the East End of London. Mostly they are cerebral palsy cases and come from seriously deprived, mixed-up and often broken homes. The doctor and physiotherapist at the schools pick out the children whom they consider are most likely to benefit from the therapy which the weekly riding sessions offer.

Generally, the children are confined to their wheelchairs. They are accustomed to being looked down upon by their elders and others. Put them on a pony and their vantage point is dramatically elevated. It is they, and not others, who now have the advantage of superior height. It offers them their only practical chance of being able to place a hand on top of an adult's head. It is this, and the independence that riding gives them (they can then cast off their wheelchairs and crutches) which offers a new outlook on life. And when there is added the contact with the ponies, and all that this means in their young lives, the effects of the therapy upon them can be profound.

The degree of the mental and physical indignity to which the children have often been subjected is barely credible. The instances are poignant in their consistency. There was the red-headed boy of ten who, when he first started coming to the Mews, wouldn't let Joan Bader – or anyone – touch him; nor would he speak. The story was that, when he was three or four, his mother had had twins, one of whom had died. After the death, the child was told by the parent that it was he who should have died because there was something wrong with him. He was an abnormal child whereas the baby was quite healthy. After that, he never spoke again either at home or at school.

After two or three weeks of riding in the indoor school, there was still no improvement. Then one day, after his ride, Joan said firmly but persuasively to him: 'Come on, touch the pony and say "thank you".'

The boy went up to the animal, gave him a pat and in a clear and distinct voice said 'thank you'. The physiotherapist could hardly credit it.

As the weeks went by his condition steadily improved. Whenever he got out of the school bus, he would run up to Joan and hug and kiss her. ('He really quite hurt.') All the while he was speaking in long and coherent sentences. The patting of the pony and the uninhibited words of gratitude had liberated his constricted mind and tongue.

Then came the depressing reverse. One afternoon when he arrived for his ride he was back where he had started. Not a word came from his mouth. The weeks of effort seemed to have come to nought. Joan asked the physiotherapist what she thought could have happened. 'Oh,' she said, 'his mother had a boyfriend staying in the house last weekend and because there was a man around the boy was ill treated as usual to make him keep quiet. It's always the same. When that happens he reverts to his old condition.'

It took three or four more weekly rides, with patting and thanking the pony at the end, before the hurt had been exorcized and the sentences began to flow again.

From Laddie Lucas's epic story of Bader: *Flying Colours* (Hutchinson/Stanley Paul)

Vidal Sassoon
Salon czar

One morning recently I was watching ABC television's 'Good Morning New York' show. Somewhere between my coffee and toast a feature came on about a stud farm in Santa Barbara, California. 'These beautiful, purebred white arabs don't look so clean and smart by accident,' said the presenter. 'No, in fact every day they are specially groomed and manicured.' Suddenly a hand reached out and sprayed a magnificent white stallion with a large commercial-sized canister of Vidal Sassoon shampoo, followed it with my conditioner and then a finishing lotion. I could hardly believe my eyes. But I must admit, he did look very special afterwards.

Gordon Richards

Horseman and knight

Sir Gordon Richards has personal memories of most of the big racing moments of this century. Like the occasion when he was a stable lad at Jimmy White's private stables at Foxhill, Wiltshire.

Playing soccer for the stable team, his side were awarded a penalty. Recalls Sir Gordon: 'I always played right-back but I wanted the left-back to take the penalty. The score was 3–3 with minutes to go.

'Mr White shouted out that if I took the penalty and scored I would be given my first ride in a proper race. I tucked the ball into the net and was duly give my first leg-up in public on Clockwork at Lingfield towards the end of 1920. We finished fourth in a nursery.

'Perhaps my funniest moment came at Leicester when a certain Captain Vivian was acting as starter for the very first time.

'At one time everybody in racing thought I was well in with all the starters, judges, the lot. This chap kept looking down at us at the start and shouting, "Are you ready, Gordon?" I was facing round the wrong way, but when he yelled out again: "Are you ready, Gordon?" Harry Wragg shouted back, "Yes, sir," and off they went.

'The rest of the field were down in the dip when I eventually got my horse round the right way and got off. Harry Wragg was always nicknamed the Head Waiter but he didn't wait that day. He fooled the starter before we even got going.'

From *Willie Carson: A Biography* by Claude Duval (Stanley Paul)

Tim Rice
Songwriting giant

I once ventured into the world of horse racing as an owner when I was persuaded by Bill, a friend of mine who made a living out of horses, to purchase one third of a beast called 'Arzam Boy'; the third third was owned by the son of a trainer. So I was assured that this was 'great news'. We entered Arzam Boy in various races and first time out he actually came fifth; next time he came ninth, then he began coming last but one and then last. Whatever he did, the trainer always said, 'He just ran a perfect race, just what I wanted.' I went all over the country watching this nag come last everywhere. Then a decision was taken to 'chop his cobblers off'. We were assured that this would speed him up a bit. I thought the threat of it would speed him up, but anyway the poor sod had his manhood removed and he was then sent 'over the sticks'.

'It was obviously clear,' said the trainer, 'that this horse wasn't a flat horse, he was only a horse for the sticks.' And he went everywhere. He went all round Britain on the jump courses, and we ended up in Hamilton or somewhere to race against two milk float horses and he still managed to come last and I had the farce of little jockeys coming up to me who were about a third of my height asking me for my advice before the race. All I was able to say was get in front and stay there.

Anyway, it came to the point after about a year of disaster, when the trainer's son who owned one third said, 'I think we ought to cut down the insurance on this horse. Because he's a bit of a loser and we're paying quite big insurance premiums.' I said 'fine' and inferred that instead of insuring him for about £2000, we should insure him for about £500, as that was what he was worth. I was about to do this and cut my premium when my friend with the second third said, 'Hang on, don't insure him for that; insure him for what you put in. Because you aren't just insuring the horse, you're insuring the whole investment. I'm insuring my third for two grand on its own.' So I went along with my mate and the other guy insured his bit for £400. So two thirds of the horse were valued at £2000 per third and the other third was valued at £400.

His disastrous run continued and after this insurance incident, he fell at Worcester. Then at Windsor the poor horse fell again and had to be put down. Consequently, Bill and I got all our money back, whereas the poor chap 'in the business' ended up with just the £400 return. I felt very guilty about it because I felt as if it might almost have been fate, and I would rather have had the horse eating grass in my field than to have fallen and have to be put down like that. So I came out of the episode with all that I had put in, but very sad, and I have never gone back to horse racing.

Diana Dors/Alan Lake
Showbiz nobility

Well, I've never really had anything to do with horses except when I bought Alan a present of a horse. A couple of months later he broke his back out riding, but perhaps he should tell you . . . .

Yeah, it was a lovely present I had when I came out of prison, called Sapphire. I'd ridden a hell of a lot before so I went out into Windsor Great Park and had a clash with the trees. Broke my back and wrecked my shoulder and generally made a mess of myself. But thank God I'm up and walking again now.

I've always loved horses, though. When I was a kid in Stoke-on-Trent, we used to go over to this one field that didn't have a factory on it and they used to have circuses there. At the end of the season, they would turn the circus ponies out to have a run, and all they did was run in circles. It was very sad.

Colonel Blashford-Snell
Adventurer

Some time ago I was working in India and my poor horse was having a terrible time at night being bitten by vampire bats. The screams from the poor horse were unbearable. I couldn't think what to do. Then my batman (sorry about that) came up with the idea of making a suit out of pink parachute material, to keep the bats off the horse. Well, it was worth a try. Sure enough we had a quiet night. Unfortunately, in the morning the horse had vanished. So we had to set out to find it. After driving for miles we came across a small Indian village in complete turmoil. The head man explained that the night before they had held a religious festival to bring luck to the village and help with the harvest. At about midnight a ghost had appeared. A wild horse in pink pyjamas had galloped through the middle of the ceremony. They were all in a terrible state of panic and fear. My poor horse had frightened them to death. In the end, after spending ages trying to pacify them and recapturing my mount, I had to give the horse to the village. Pyjamas and all.

Alan Ball

Pelotalist

Alan had a decent horse; it had been third and second amongst a fair class and he wanted a really good opinion on it. So he thought, who better to ride it than Lester Piggott, the King! Come the big day and Alan thought to himself, well, I'll find out now. So he and the trainer put Lester up on to this horse and off it goes in the race. It didn't run a bad race at all, finishing just out of the frame, fourth. Alan scuttled down to see Lester afterwards, keen to get an opinion as to how decent the horse was and feeling quietly confident. He ran up just as Lester was dismounting and enthused, 'What did you think? Do you think there's any future in her? What did she run like?' Lester summed it up in one word.

'Glue.'

Liz Emanuel
Haute couturier

I used to have this little pony called 'Windy', and it was about two weeks before a very important county show, when we were trying to qualify for Wembley. Oops! I'll get into trouble now. He was out in the field and he rubbed his tail or maybe another pony chewed it or something. So he was just left with this stump with a couple of straggly hairs hanging off the end. A really revolting sight. We were desperate. So we got this wig maker, who normally just does wigs for people, to make a tail for Windy. To create the tail we had to get a few of the remaining hairs from Windy and match them up. It was quite an amazing job and we had to plait it into his own tail; you couldn't actually tell in the end that it was a false one.

Then at the show we were riding around and suddenly he just stood there, and another pony came up behind him and started chewing away. Pulled the wig off in the middle of the show ring! And we were standing right in front of the judges.

Barry Sheene

Bionic world motorcycle champion

Boody 'orses. I 'ate 'em. I've only ever been on 'em twice, and both times they nearly wrote me off.

Mrs David Broome

David Broome's wife

We've got one little boy who's four years old. Once David took him upstairs and put him into bed, which is a very rare occurrence, as David is never normally home to put him to bed, and he was reading him a story, and doing fatherly things; and he said, 'Right, James, tomorrow we are going to do something together. Just you and I, as I don't spend much time with you. So what do you think we should do?' Little Jamie sat and had a little think, and he said, 'Well, I'm gonna ride my pony tomorrow, Daddy.' Now, this is quite uncommon because James has to be handcuffed and forced to get on his pony. David, absolutely over the moon, said, 'Well, that's lovely James. Great.' 'Yes,' said James. 'And I'm gonna ride him first thing in the morning.' David thought, My God, he's really keen. This is fantastic. 'Yes,' James carried on. 'Then we'll get it over and done with for the day.'

Alex Higgins

Ace of the green baize

I decided to become a jockey because I had all the necessary qualifications: I'd always been keen on horses, and I weighed 7 stone. I got a telephone number from somebody and went along to Eddie Reavey's stables near Wantage in Berkshire, for a sort of trial. Not that I dreamed of winning the Grand National or anything like that, as I'd no horsy background. But there are two ways to upset me, even now. One is to insult Muhammad Ali and the other is to criticize Lester Piggott. I've never missed an opportunity of watching them in action, to see their adrenalin flow and how they're the masters of it. They are supreme. They have the knowledge. In horse racing you might only feel that adrenalin for a few minutes; in snooker it can be steadily pumping through your whole body for three hours. But whatever the sport, it's like high-octane fuel. It's a drug. You feel super big, and once you've had that feeling, you get it where you can. I suppose, at fifteen, I thought I might get it from flat racing.

As it turned out, I never had a public ride. The most exhilarating thing that happened to me all the time I was at the stables was that I got into a few fights. They were the same size as me, these lads, and I thumped a couple of them that deserved it. There's a hierarchy in stables from the apprentice jockey down to the stable boy. I was the stable boy. I shovelled the crap. Well, the assistant head lad was seven or eight years older and any time Reavey thought he had a good horse on his hands, this assistant head lad would be the one to look after it. It must have turned his head, because he used to order the rest of us about something shocking. One night it was pouring with rain, and I'd had just about enough of this Little Hitler malarky, so I decided to put him straight on a few points. I set about him in the courtyard. They had to pull me off. This was the first outbreak of an allergy I have, to being ordered about.

Reavey didn't know what went on, really, or if he did he turned a blind eye to it. On another occasion – it was nine o'clock at night in the middle of winter, and pitch dark – I was riding a bicycle with no brakes, heading back from the shops, when suddenly what should appear on the hill 50 yards from the stables, crossing the road, but the local bobby. Smack, I hit him. I came off the bike, and he was on the deck, so I ran round the back of a barn and took the long way home. They traced the bike back to the stables, but to this day they don't know who was riding it. All they know is, it wasn't Lester Piggott.

I remember some of the jockeys at the stables. There was Willie Currie who alas no longer rides: he rode second in the £10,000 News of the World Handicap fifteen years ago and that was a big, big race. The kid just didn't have the strength to ride the horse out. I remember Pat Reavey too: a tragedy that he never fulfilled his destiny. He'd be about twenty-six now.

So much depends on the rides you get, because a terrible jockey can win on a good horse. I have a jockey friend in Ireland who was a champion apprentice but he's still breaking his heart trying to get rides. You've got to be something really special, and even then for the first six years you're crucified with training and weight problems. I don't think I could have stood breakfasting on a cigar like Piggott, or having two boiled eggs for Christmas dinner. Or taking pee pills and what have you like a lot of them do. I put on weight. After starving myself to death in Belfast, here I was having breakfast at 8.30, dinner at one, tea at six, and getting a lot of fresh air. My weight soared from 7 stone or 7.7 to 9.10 and 10 stone. So I was out. Besides, Eddie Reavey didn't think much of my stable boy abilities. Not to mince matters, he said I was useless. That I was a lazy bum. He was a fair judge, because although I liked the riding, I didn't rate the chores and the mucking out: I used to be a shirker. Still, I was choked when Reavey died. I didn't know what to put on the wreath. He was sixty-odd, and cancer got him, but when I knew him he was a great trainer, somebody who all but had the National sewn up if the horse hadn't had a mind of its own. It's a hard world.

From *Hurricane Higgins' Snooker Scrapbook* by Alex Higgins and Angela Patmore (Souvenir Press)

Roger Moore
007

When I made *Ivanhoe*, I had a wonderful grey whose name was Shane. He had started in the film world in *Richard III* and worked much better after a packet of Polos. His favourite trick was being a camera hog. He always sensed where the camera was and would go to the centre of frame. It was a marvellous thing for an actor to have a horse like that. I knew I would be in centre picture too, because Shane was there. He trod on everyone's feet getting there, but fortunately he couldn't tread on mine.

Jack Leach

Favourite former jockey

I have certainly met many racegoers who were not quite normal and one of them was Jack Robinson, who trained for Cunliffe and Purefoy (the Hermits of Druid's Lodge).

Robinson was a very bad-tempered man, especially early in the morning. Every day when he went out on the Downs with his first string of horses he used to hold his handkerchief up in the air and swear. One morning his jockey said to him: 'Excuse me, Mr Robinson, surely the wind cannot always be in the wrong direction.' 'Yes, it is,' said Robinson. 'If it is in the north it is bad for the horses, and if it is in the south or west it is bad for my pigs. And if it's in the east it's bad for me.' Robinson had a shelter made up on the Downs and the stable boys called it the governor's unrest.

There is another story about Jack Robinson. After the first lot had completed the gallops, he jumped off his hack and left it standing outside the office. He went inside and left the door open. At this juncture one of the apprentices happened to pass by and, being slightly curious about the result, whacked the horse across the rump. The hack leaped into the room and, as the linoleum was freshly polished, fell down. I do not know if you have ever had a horse jump into a small room and fall down. It takes up a considerable amount of space. Jack Robinson left by the window so that the horse would have all the space he needed. The hack slipped and skidded and finally, getting halfway up, fell back out of the door on to less slippery ground. Robinson came round the building, remounted and rode away. They say it was the first and only time in his life he was at a loss for words.

From *Heard in the Paddock* edited by Roderick Bloomfield (Stanley Paul)

Wayne Sleep
Dashing high stepper

When asked if he'd ever had an experience with a horse, Wayne just replied, 'Oooh!'

W. Smith

Royal jockey

I'd just come in off a ride for the Queen Mother and as I was loosening the girth of my horse it stood on my foot. My boots were made of very soft lightweight leather and I shouted 'F...' at the top of my voice and turned around to look straight into the face of Her Royal Highness. I spent the next ten minutes praying silently and babbling on about how wonderful her horse was. And as she walked away, I leant into the horse and removed my toe from under its foot.

Peter O'Sullevan

Saddling discloser

On the sunlit afternoon of 6 June 1982, against the impressive backcloth of the Château de Chantilly, the Irish-trained challenger for the French Derby, Assert, was to attempt the first breach in the home defence in the 145 years' history of the Prix du Jockey Club.

The O'Brien clan's first impact on the Gallic scene – sequel to a peaceful nineteenth-century invasion of the region of Bordeaux – is still happily reflected in bottles labelled Haut Brion. Not a few were broached in the mid-twentieth century when the renowned Tipperary trainer Vincent O'Brien sent Ballymoss to Paris to win the Prix de l'Arc de Triomphe in the sensitive hands of Scobie Breasley.

In the seventies, Vincent was to win two more Arcs but the nearest he had come to winning France's premier classic – vainly tackled by generations of English and Irish challengers – was the half length runner-up, Artaius, in 1977.

Now his son David, twenty-six, loyally standing by the stable jockey, Christy Roche, despite his relative inexperience of French racing conditions, was bidding to amend the records with a horse bought as a yearling at current bargain basement rates (£15,000) under the very noses of France's top experts as well as the representatives of multi-millionaire oil and tanker tycoons in the Goff's-France sales complex adjacent to Longchamp racecourse.

For the second time in television history the race was to be relayed 'live' from the Cité du Cheval to British screens.

Only when the *tiercé* (1, 2, 3 forecast) is harnessed to a race does it receive full coverage in French newspapers. So a classic contest featuring the best quality in Europe may be totally ignored if the *tiercé* is associated with a mediocre handicap on the same programme.

On this occasion the mammoth weekly gamble, indulged by countless Frenchmen who wager up to 125 million francs in units of 5 francs in seeking to name the first three in correct order, was associated with the Jockey Club.

Among the thirty-seven principal national newspapers, twenty-six risked a charge of treason by naming Assert their first choice; eight championed the cause of Cadoudal who had won two of his three races and was thought to have been very unlucky in defeat.

There were single votes for Bois de Grâce (representative of six times successful Cantilien veteran François Mathet), Alfred's Choice and Japanese-owned, American-bred Real Shadai. England's representative, Criterion, was as friendless as an importer of Canterbury lamb.

Following recent rain, the well-manicured bright green turf would surely be perfect for all 14 runners. The almost cloudless sky mocked the meterological threat of electric disturbance.

Visibility was perfect. It should have been a commentator's dream. But this race interpreter could not dispel the nightmare of the corresponding day in 1981.

Then, the commentary point had been 'set up' on a corner of the photographers' eerie, a narrow grandstand roof-top parapet. The little museum-piece of a monitor, unequipped with any sort of shield against direct daylight on an open roof, was clearly going to be useless. And my photographer friends indicated with regretful Gallic shrugs that as soon as the field swung into the three furlongs straight they would be obliged to lean out with their zoom lenses and totally obscure my vision. In the event, they were not exaggerating.

That nice Monsieur Romanet pointed out later that the BBC 'site' had been on a lower tier. Next year there would be a proper commentary box on that level. He was right, there was. But, understandably, it was tenanted by my French colleague, André Théron. And on 6 June 1982 the same little useless monitor and several kilometres of comprehensively scrambled cables were back in the corner of the roof-top parapet.

I had confirmed the worst an hour since when meeting the BBC's experienced floor manager Mike Ross on ground level.

In the tones of one inured to the impediments with which overseas racing telecasts are invariably bedevilled, he announced resignedly, 'We've got problems.'

I said I realized that, having only lately descended from the roof. 'No, not that,' he countered, lightly dismissing so normal a triviality as a disastrous commentary point. 'We have no lines!'

The intention was for French TV cameras to provide coverage of first the 3.30 (2.30 English time) which 'BBC Grandstand' would receive direct and over which I would commentate. Then London would return to us for the big one, due off at 4.20.

Frantic parleys ensued between the French engineer, hired by the BBC for the occasion, the technician attached to the French TV service, and the French Post Office.

The *responsable* at the Bureau de Poste regretted that the combination of Premiers Margaret Thatcher and François Mitterand meeting at Versailles and the French Open Tennis Championship had absorbed all circuits. One could become available – but it was impossible to predict when.

There was still an hour to transmission – or non-transmission.

As at Epsom on Derby Day, signs of recession were markedly absent. More and more tables were pressed into service in the open air, tree-shaded main enclosure restaurant which served a 300 francs menu *boisson non compris*.

I crossed the course to the picnic area, bought a couple of freshly barbecued spicy sausages and a very passable glass of wine for a total of 20 francs and reflected on the striking difference in ambience between Chantilly (30 miles from Paris) and Epsom (15 miles outside London).

Supporters of Britain's licensing laws should visit both regions on Derby Day and consider the grounds for *la différence*.

The runners for 'Grandstand's' first race of the day had not only cantered to the post but were entering the stalls when, in the continued absence of a circuit, the technicians finally achieved a link by telephone.

The London producer understandably opted for a recording rather than 'live' feed into the programme. '*Je n'ai pas de micro*,' I called anxiously to the technical wizard as the last horse was installed.

He threw one three feet – and we were in business!

Maybe it would be better for the big one which 'Grandstand' now said they would definitely take live through the telephone.

Then the weather decided to keep faith with the met. forecast. The cables which entwined our feet crackled ominously as forked lightning heralded a sudden monsoon. The little monitor packed up completely.

John Hanmer returning from his second 75-flight scamper to obtain news of the latest betting was shouting it down the phone to the London studio. They weren't hearing too good they said! Would Mike Moss come on the line? Nice, I thought, they're going to leave us here to be electrocuted while they stay with the tiddley-winks . . . Wrong again. 'They're coming to you in three minutes,' called Mike. 'Julian is just reading the runners and . . .' His voice was drowned by the sudden exultant cry of Monsieur Albert – we were on *cher ami* terms by now – announcing, '*Nous avons un circui!*'

Albert and his mate had 2 minutes 40 seconds to change all the wiring. When they plugged in my headset I heard '. . . O'Sullevan at the course'. And, wondering what viewers were seeing via the rented Regional cameras (all RTF's top equipment was deployed at the tennis) said, 'Good afternoon and welcome to Chantilly . . .'

Marcao, ridden by the young American Cash Asmussen, led early on from Criterion, Newdjar, Real Shadai and Bois de Grâce.

Assert's trainer and jockey had flown over the week before to study in detail every gradient of the circuit. They decided that wherever the horse was drawn (and, in the event, he drew a favourable low number on the inside) they would make for the 'outer' even though it meant covering more ground than necessary – to avoid any possible interference.

By the time the runners reached the point passing the magnificent stables of the Chateau, Christy had neatly found his pitch.

As he eased round the outside of the leaders entering the home stretch (by which time he was in fourth position), I eased out over the parapet to keep him in my sights.

I was conscious of the cry of one of my photographer friends '*Attention, Peter. La descente est rapide.*' But more so of Assert's irresistible victory surge and, as I called him home, the words over my headset (maybe they were hearing me after all?) from London, 'Repeat the first four and stop talking.'

Mike Moss ('I've been in some traumatic situations but that was far and away my worst experience ever') looked all of ten years older.

It was a great win and Chantilly is a fine racecourse. But for working conditions give me Sedgefield any day!

Harry Llewellyn
Olympian

I lay on my bed, staring desperately at the white wall of my room and repeating over and over again, 'I must go to sleep – I must go to sleep.' And, eventually, I slept.

A few hours later I rode out of the Helsinki Stadium knowing that with Foxhunter's final effortless clear round the British team had won my country's only gold medal at the Summer Olympics of 1952. Somehow Foxhunter understood my elation as, with ears pricked, he trotted gaily from the arena.

Foxhunter and I had an extraordinary affinity. I think, on looking back, this is why I understood him so well. I knew when he was not feeling well; I knew when he had a headache. He loathed it when it was hot; and he told me so. Very few things upset him. He was a very calm horse after a competition; I never saw him put his ears back. He was the most extraordinarily docile animal and this endeared him to so many people, and he had those big, beautiful, soft-brown eyes.

I used to talk to him a lot, either to wake him up or settle him down and he understood me very well. In fact he understood me so well that if I wanted to stop I would very often find that he did stop. If I wanted him to check I suppose I must have done something very slight; but at even a very slight touch he would check – he would check to a standstill. At a show in aid of the Commonwealth Games in 1958 we were asked to give an exhibition. I brought him up off grass and he was asked to jump a few little four-foot fences to show the art of control – gallop on, stop, turn sharp left, turn sharp right, jump the fences at an angle and stop. This was two or three years after he had retired and he was just as good as he ever was.

Tom Brake who was watching and who was one of the original

team that went to Nice and Rome in 1947 – we called ourselves 'The Guinea Pigs' – came up to me afterwards and said, 'You know, we will never see the like of that again.'

Colin Varder of the *Daily Express* said that Foxhunter was so clever that he could sign his own autograph, and as a result I had thousands of letters. I could not discover what letters were for me and what was fan mail. Eventually I had to get three girls down at the paper's expense to go through suitcases of letters separating my own from those intended for Foxhunter. Eventually the *Daily Express* put a stop to it and they printed a copy of my signature inside one of his so-called 'hoofprints' and sent them to all Foxhunter fans.

Then again, there was his appearance. He was a fine-looking, very big horse. He always had his ears pricked and looked as if he enjoyed life. He was just under seventeen hands and he had a majestic way of cantering into the ring. Mike Ansell drew attention to the fact that in France Foxhunter was often referred to as 'Monseigneur', and he was certainly referred to in the press as 'Monseigneur Foxhunter'. He had this sort of charisma which showed him up either as a great aristocrat or a great film star. His appearance was very much in his favour and this, combined with his skill and gentle nature made him something quite different.

On one occasion at Harringay he was looking around him in the ring when he suddenly spied a little grey wall. It was a funny little fence with holes in it. I believe horses are colour-blind and the density of the colour of this wall was almost the density of the colour of the track. When he suddenly came to this wall he stopped. I turned him round, scolded him and tapped him down the shoulder twice. My goodness me! There was complete silence. People had enough manners in those days not to boo, but I had many letters saying that I was not to do that – in fact I had one saying, 'You must not hit Foxhunter because he does not belong to you he belongs to the nation'! I had to be very careful not even to speak crossly to him after that. He was the chap they liked – not me. I was not a national hero, but he was.

Foxhunter died at the age of nineteen on 28 November 1959, having done something to himself in the field. He was perfectly well when he was put out to grass but he was rather apt to buck around and mess about and I think he must have injured himself falling when jumping the ditch in the middle of our park field. He died of a ruptured artery to his kidneys and went very quickly. I was at home when it happened and saw he kept on going down. He was brought in and the vet, Ken Mitchell, was there almost immediately. He noted from the colour of Foxhunter's gums that there was little or no blood supply to his head. He said he was dying and soon life left that magnificent body. He left us peacefully and without pain. You cannot say he died in my arms but I was holding his head when he died. He had been a great friend to me and to many others who were so fond of him.

I did not tell anybody for a few days, by which time I could talk about him without a continuous lump in my throat. I was to remember how joyfully he had cooperated with his human friends and put so much pleasure into our lives.

Shortly after Foxhunter died we decided upon his burial. I own some land situated on the top of the Blorenge mountain over-looking both Gobion and Llanvair Grange; and on my property right at the top are some rocks. Here we found a cavity into which we put a stainless-steel casket. In this was placed the book I had written, *Foxhunter in Pictures*, and his hide, which we had brought back from the kennels where he had been taken after his death. His skeleton was carefully preserved and this was asked for by the Royal Veterinary College; it still stands there next door to the statue of Hermit, a famous racehorse who won the Snowstorm Derby in 1867.

Some people have asked why I left his skeleton there but buried him elsewhere. The answer is simple. In the Royal Veterinary College his skeleton will be a constant reminder of a great horse, while the burial on Blorenge mountain will remind many people that he was partly trained in this beautiful country of Wales. The Blorenge gives wonderful views of about seventy miles in every direction; it is a lovely place for him to be buried. We often exercised over that spot; and the thought of this great horse buried there means a great deal to me.

From *Passports to Life* by Harry Llewellyn (Stanley Paul)